Look for Pepper

Written by Jan Burchett and Sara Vogler
Illustrated by Begoña Corbalan

Collins

Pepper is not on her chair.

2

Pepper is not on my coat.

We will look for her.

4

I need a torch.

I see a tail.

It is Buzz.

Is that Pepper hidden?

No, that is an owl.

Is Pepper under the arch?

No, that is a rubbish bag.

I can hear Pepper.

13

Look for Pepper

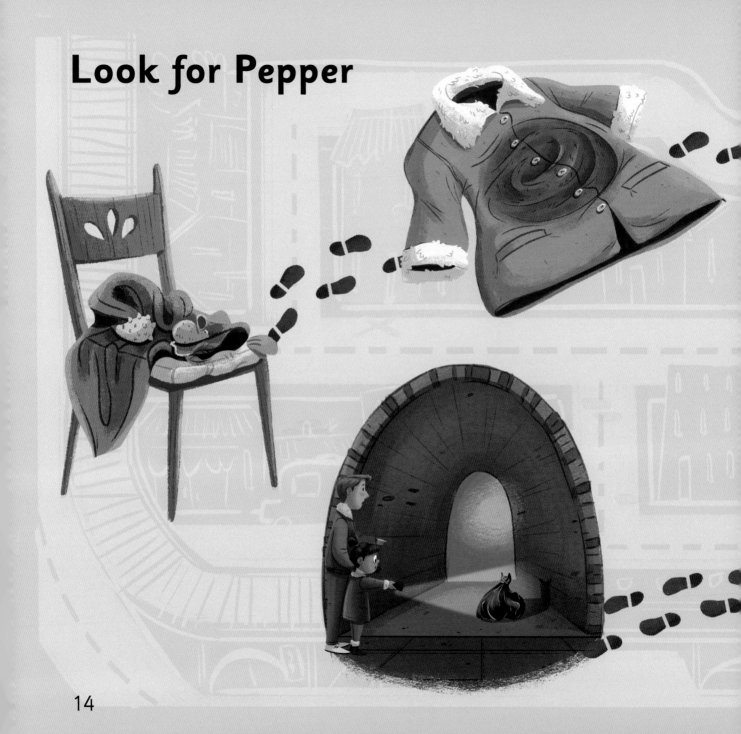

🐾 Review: After reading 🐾

Use your assessment from hearing the children read to choose any GPCs, words or tricky words that need additional practice.

Read 1: Decoding

- Turn to page 5. Discuss the meaning of **need** and explain how it is different to 'want'. (*'need' means must have*) Ask: Why does the girl **need** a torch? (*she can't see in the dark without it*)
- Ask the children to sound out these words. Ask: Which two letters make one sound?
  hidden (*dd*) **coat** (*oa*) **owl** (*ow*) **look** (*oo*) **see** (*ee*)
- Point to the following words and ask: Can you blend in your head when you read these words? Then, challenge the children to read the words out loud.
  Pepper (page 2) **chair** (page 2) **arch** (page 10) **rubbish** (page 11) **hear** (page 12)

Read 2: Prosody

- Turn to page 8 and point to the question mark. Ask children to demonstrate reading the sentence like a question.
- Focus on page 9 and point to the comma. Explain how this breaks up the answer, **No** and the explanation of what it is.
- Ask children to demonstrate reading the sentence on page 9, pausing at the comma.

Read 3: Comprehension

- Ask the children if they have ever lost anything. Did they look in the same places as the girl or in different places? Did they find the missing thing easily or was it difficult, like in the book?
- Look together through pages 6 to 11, asking what they thought Pepper was. Ask:
  - Why did they keep making a mistake? (*things look different in the dark*)
  - Ask: What looked like a cat under the arch? (*a rubbish bag*)
  - Ask the children to describe shadows and shapes in the dark that they have seen, and what they really were.
- Look together at pages 14 and 15.
  - Ask the children to use the pictures to help them retell the story in sequence.
  - Ask them to talk with a partner about what might happen if Pepper goes missing another time. Where would they look for her? Where would they find her? What would happen in the end?